PARAKEETS

BY KATHRYN STEVENS

The Child's World®

Published by The Child's World®
1980 Lookout Drive • Mankato, MN 56003-1705
800-599-READ • www.childsworld.com

Acknowledgments
The Child's World®: Mary Berendes, Publishing Director
The Design Lab: Design
Michael Miller: Editing
Sarah Miller: Editing

Photo Credits
© Africa Studio/Shutterstock.com: cover, 2, 6, 20 (food);
akrp/iStockphoto.com: 5; Alex_Schmidt/iStockphoto.com: 16;
edfuentesg/iStockphoto.com: 11; GlobalP/iStockphoto.com: 4,
19, 21, 22; Heathse/Dreamstime.com: 7; jgroup/iStockphoto.
com: 23; Juniors Bildarchiv GmbH/Alamy: 14, 15; Lusyaya/
iStockphoto.com: 8; Olikvrn/Dreamstime.com: 13; panbazil/
Shutterstock.com: back cover, cover, 1, 2 (bird), 24; Serega/
iStockphoto.com: 3; Sjonja/iStockphoto.com: 17; Smileyjoanne/
iStockphoto.com: 9; Stephen Denness/Dreamstime.com: 18

ISBN: 9781631437304
LCCN: 2014959752

Printed in the United States of America
Mankato, MN
July, 2015
PA02262

NOTE TO PARENTS AND EDUCATORS

This Pet Care series is written for children who want to be part of the pet experience but are too young to be in charge of pets without adult supervision. These books are intended to provide a kid-friendly supplement to more detailed information adults need to know about choosing and caring for different types of pets. Adults can help youngsters learn how to live happily with the animals in their lives and, with adults' help and supervision, can grow into responsible animal caretakers later on.

CONTENTS

PARAKEETS AS PETS

Parakeets are fun pets! But getting a parakeet is a big decision. Many live to be 10 to 15 years old. They need someone to care for them the whole time. These tiny animals are easily hurt. They need to be kept safe.

Parakeets pay close attention to the things around them.

Loud noises and quick movements scare parakeets. This owner is being gentle and quiet.

GOOD FOOD

Parakeets need foods that keep them healthy. They need birdseed or **pellets**. They love fruit, vegetables, and greens, too. Parakeets also need to eat sand or grit! It helps grind up the foods they eat. And they need clean water to drink.

Parakeets like to eat tiny millet seeds.

Pet stores sell special foods for parakeets. Some of the foods we eat are good for parakeets, too. This parakeet is eating fruit.

This cage has lots of room inside. The wires are close together, too. That keeps the bird from getting its head stuck.

A SAFE HOME

A parakeet needs a safe cage with lots of room. The cage should be in an area without **drafts**. It should have dishes for food and water. It needs wooden **perches** where the parakeet can stand. Swings, ladders, or rings are nice, too!

This wooden perch is safe for the bird's feet. Perches of different sizes keep the parakeet's feet strong.

FRIENDLY BIRDS

In the wild, parakeets live in large, friendly groups. Pet parakeets are friendly with people they trust. Some pet parakeets live alone. They need their human families for company. Many people keep more than one parakeet. The parakeets are happier together!

These two parakeets keep each other company. They are best friends for life!

GOOD HEALTH

Parakeets love to fly. It is great exercise!

Flying keeps the birds healthy and strong.

They can fly around the room for exercise.

But they still need to be kept safe. They

should not be left alone while they fly.

Parakeets like to stretch and flap their wings, even when they are not flying.

Sometimes parakeets need to go to an animal doctor, or **vet**. If their beak or claws get too long, the vet can trim them. Parakeets also need to chew on things. They chew on branches, cuttlebones, and special blocks.

A vet is making sure this parakeet is healthy.

This cuttlebone is from a squid-like cuttlefish. Parakeets love to chew on cuttlebones.

PLAYTIME

Parakeets are smart. They love to **explore**.

Most parakeets like to play with toys. They like to climb and take things apart. There are lots of fun bird toys to buy. Others are easy to make. Just be sure the toys are safe!

Parakeets love ladders, bells, and other toys.

This parakeet is looking at herself in a mirror.

17

This parakeet enjoys sitting on its owner's shoulder.

LOTS OF LOVE!

Parakeets do not cuddle like dogs or cats. They do not like to be held or petted. But they enjoy being close to people they trust. Some parakeets like to sit on people's shoulders. They perch on people's fingers. They chirp happily in people's ears!

This parakeet thinks his owner's finger makes a great perch!

NEEDS AND DANGERS

NEEDS:

- a nice cage
- good food to eat
- bird sand to swallow
- clean water
- safe perches
- a swing or ladder
- a mirror or other toys

DANGERS:

- cold drafts
- cats and some other animals
- smoke and cooking smells
- household cleaners and sprays
- some houseplants
- chocolate, avocados, rhubarb
- open windows

FUN FACTS

CERE:
Male parakeets have bright ceres. Females' ceres are brown.

EYES:
Parakeets see very well.

BEAK:
Parakeets' beaks grow all the time. Chewing keeps them short.

FEATHERS:
Parakeets' body feathers are very soft.

WING:
Parakeets' wing feathers are straight and stiff.

TAIL:
Parakeets' tails have long, straight feathers.

GLOSSARY

drafts (DRAFTS) Drafts are movements of cold air.

explore (ek-SPLOR) To explore is to go to new places or try new things.

pellets (PEH-lutz) Pellets are little, hard balls of something, such as animal food.

perches (PUR-chez) Perches are sticks or bars where birds can stand.

vet (VET) A vet is a doctor who takes care of animals. "Vet" is short for "veterinarian" (vet-rih-NAYR-ee-un).

TO FIND OUT MORE

BOOKS:

Kawa, Katie. *Playful Parakeets.* New York, NY: Gareth Stevens, 2011.

Macaulay, Kelley, and Bobbie Kalman. *Parakeets.* New York, NY: Crabtree, 2005.

VIDEO/DVD:

Paws, Claws, Feathers & Fins: A Kid's Guide to Happy, Healthy Pets. Goldhil Learning Series (Video 1993, DVD 2005).

WEB SITES:

Visit our Web page for lots of links about pet care:
www.childsworld.com/links

Note to parents, teachers, and librarians: We routinely verify our Web links to make sure they are safe, active sites—so encourage your readers to check them out!

INDEX

ABOUT THE AUTHOR

Kathryn Stevens has authored and edited many books for young readers, including books on animals ranging from grizzly bears to fleas. She's a lifelong pet lover and currently cares for a big, huggable pet-therapy dog named Fudge.